Crockle Saves the Ark

Written and Illustrated by
John Ryan

It was going to rain for forty days and forty nights. Mr Noah had said so and Mr Noah knew. He had built a huge Ark and put into it a pair of every kind of animal on earth so that all would live through the Great Flood which was to come. Noah also brought his wife Mrs Noah,

his two elder sons Shem and Ham and their wives, his youngest son Jaffet and Jaffet's friend Jannet. And the children had brought their pet baby crocodile called Crockle. He was extra and shouldn't have been there at all, but Ham had left a bung-hole open in the side of the Ark for him to slip through.

The day after the rain started to fall, gloomy Mr and Mrs Shem

and happy Mr and Mrs Ham

and Jaffet and Jannet

and Crockle, who was pretending not to be there,

and all the animals

settled down to wait for the Ark to float.

High in his special observation cabin, Mr Noah was busy with his maps and instruments. Being rather absent-minded he had forgotten that the maps would be useless when the water covered all the land.

At the other end of the room, sensible Mrs Noah was watering the seedlings and herbs and the flowers and vegetables which she knew would come in useful when the Great Flood was over. 'Time to take a peep outside,' said Mr Noah.

'Yes indeed,' he added, opening the window, 'the water's getting pretty deep.' And looking down *inside* the Ark he called:

'Everything and everyone shipshape?'

Jaffet and Jannet couldn't understand what he was talking about.

None of the animals looked much like the shape of a ship,

although Crockle did his very best to try.

Nay children, that's not what "shipshape" means.

said Ham, who happened to be passing.

'It means "secure" and "waterproof" and all set up for the voyage.'

'Let's go out on deck and have a look.'

But when they got outside and looked they had a shock;

for although the water was rising fast

the Ark wasn't!

Mr Noah and the others joined them.

Just then everyone heard a loud splashing noise coming from *inside* the Ark. They ran in to look,

and deep down at the bottom of the great hull they saw a strange sight.

The hippos and the seals and the walruses and the sea-lions and all the other water-loving animals . . .

and quite a few of the birds were having a swim. And the Ark was filling up with water!

'There must be a leak!' cried Ham. 'How can we find it?' asked Jaffet.

'Let's send Crockle down to inspect,' suggested Jannet. 'He's clever and he's good at swimming under water.' A moment later Crockle dived into the water and disappeared.

He was gone for some time. People were just starting to get worried . . .

when they heard Mrs Ham shouting: 'There he is! He's in the water *outside* the Ark!' 'How did he get out?' asked Jaffet. 'Same way as he got in I expect,' said Ham. 'Through that bung-hole near the keel. The water's coming *in* because the *bung's* come out.' 'And there it is!' called Jannet. 'Fetch it Crockle!'

And because Crockle was a clever young crocodile he knew just what to do.

He seized the bung in his teeth and dived down with it,

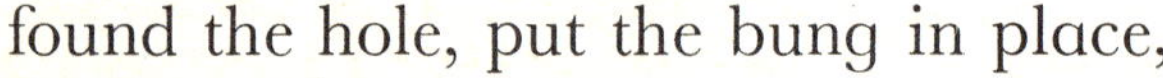

found the hole, put the bung in place,

hammered it home with his snout and swam up to the surface again.

Crockle was tired and needed to be helped on board the Ark again. 'Well done!' called Jannet as they pulled him up.

'We'd have all been drowned without him,' cried Jaffet. 'Three cheers for Crockle!' And all the animals inside the Ark joined in.

They cheered and roared and barked and grunted and growled and howled and chirped.

‘But now,’ said Mr Noah, ‘if we’re going to get the Ark afloat, we must get rid of all the water inside.’

So then, although some of the animals were sorry to lose their swimming pool, everybody began to help. For the elephants with their trunks it was easy.

The giraffes used their long necks like cranes to lift up buckets full of water and to empty them over the side of the Ark.

The rhinos and hippos worked a special seesaw pump which Ham had invented, and all the different kinds of monkey joined in and got in everybody's way.

The cat family kept well out of the way because they all hated water.

Last of all the family put on their gumboots, made a chain and passed up bucket after bucket . . .

to Ham who poured them over the side until every drop of water that had been inside was outside,

and the Ark was
afloat at last.

Then everybody made a fuss of Crockle because he had been so clever, and Shem even gave him half a ship's biscuit.

Although Mr Noah pretended not to see Crockle because he already had two perfectly good (or perfectly bad) crocodiles on board the Ark.

That evening everybody went out to see how the Great Flood was getting on. It was still raining hard. The land was quickly changing into sea. Only a few islands here and there were left.

'And very soon there will be no land at all,' said Mr Noah. 'I knew it,' said gloomy Mrs Shem. 'We shall be adrift for ever and ever!'

But then Mrs Ham brought out hot steaming cocoa and everybody, Mrs Shem included, began to feel much better.

'I think it's going to be fun,' said Jannet. 'I don't mind *how* long we stay on the Ark.' 'Hear hear!' said Jaffet, and Crockle gave a little grunt to show that he was happy too.